COOL!

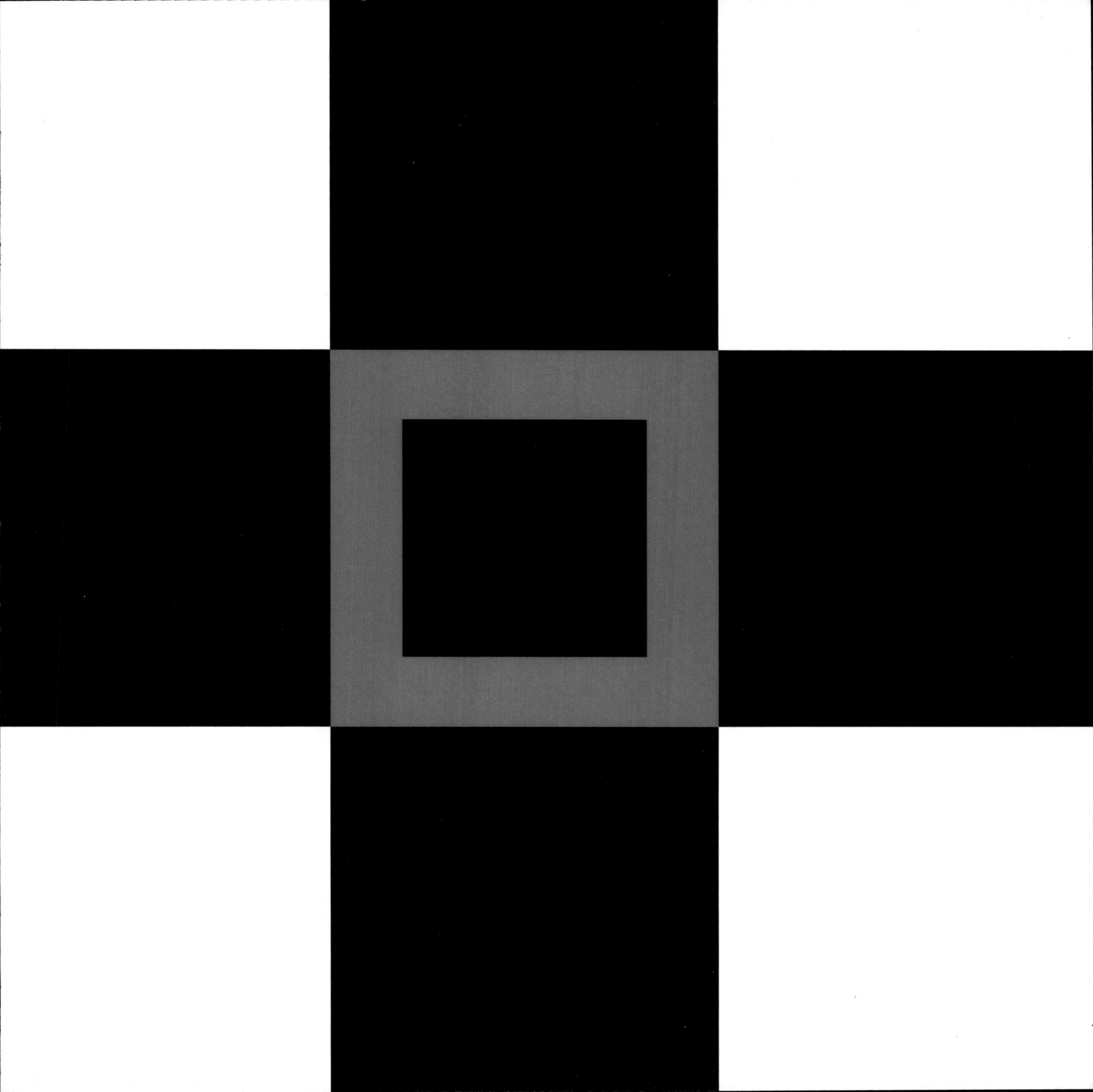

SUPER

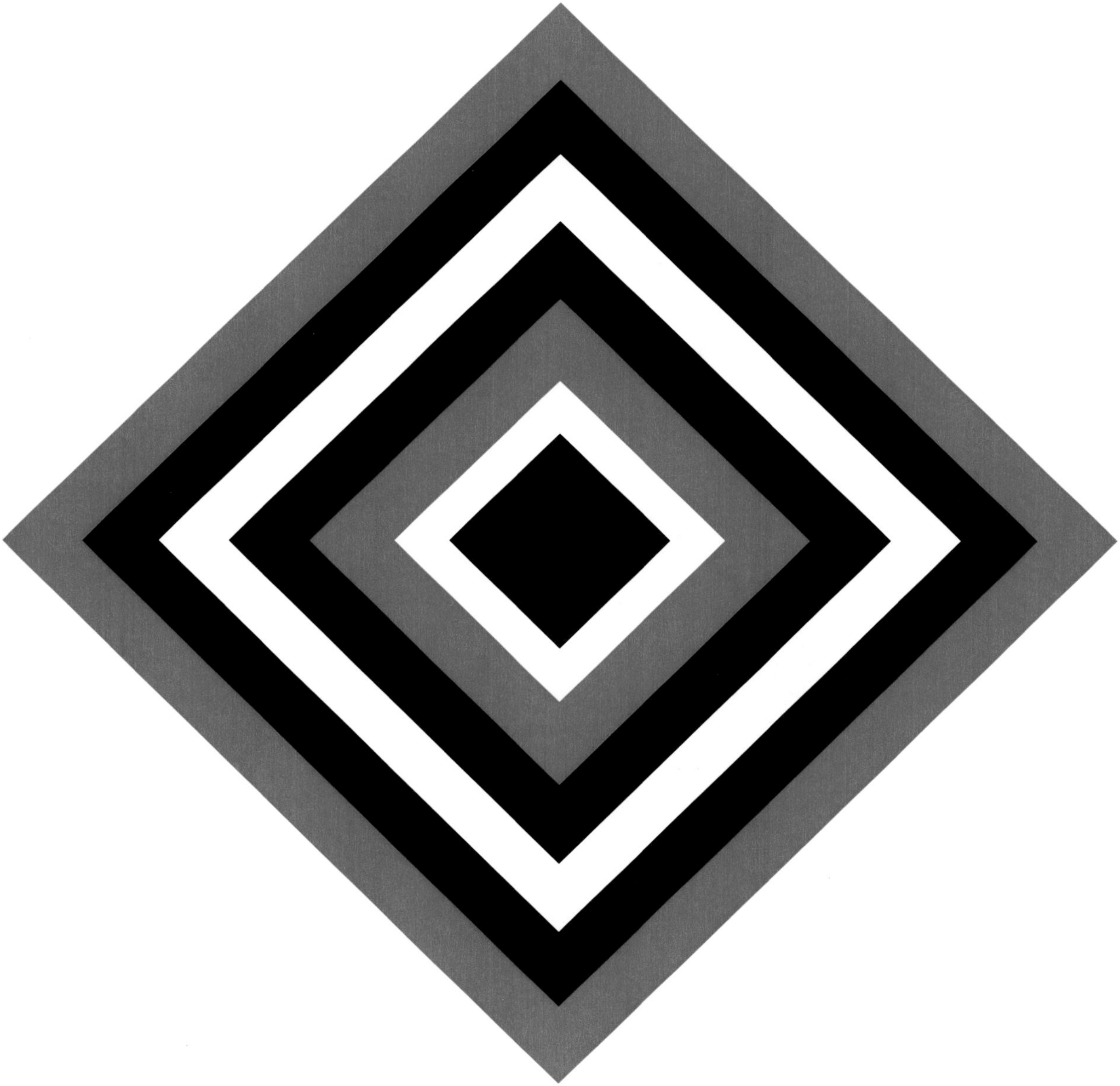

Baseball

WOW

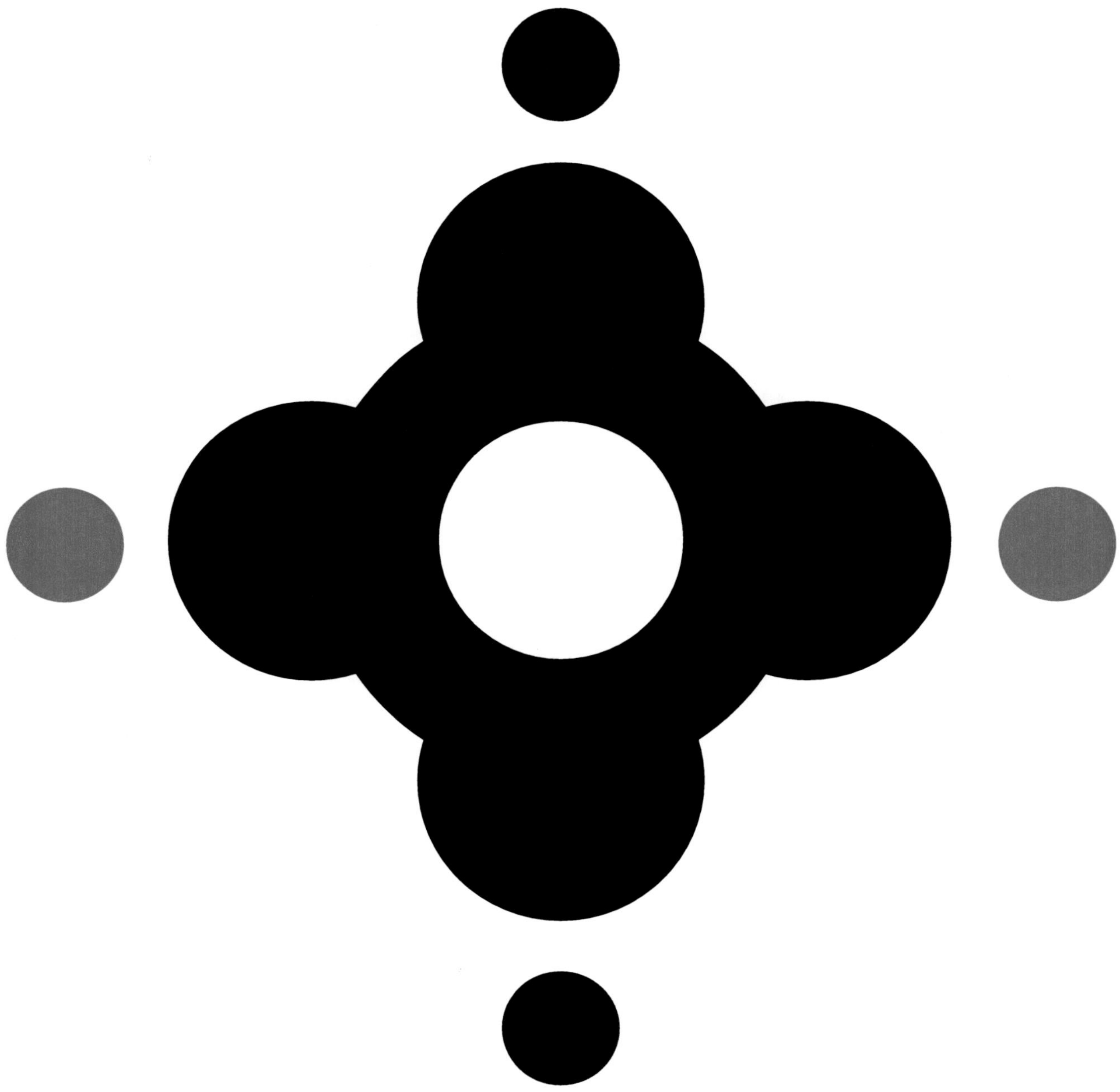

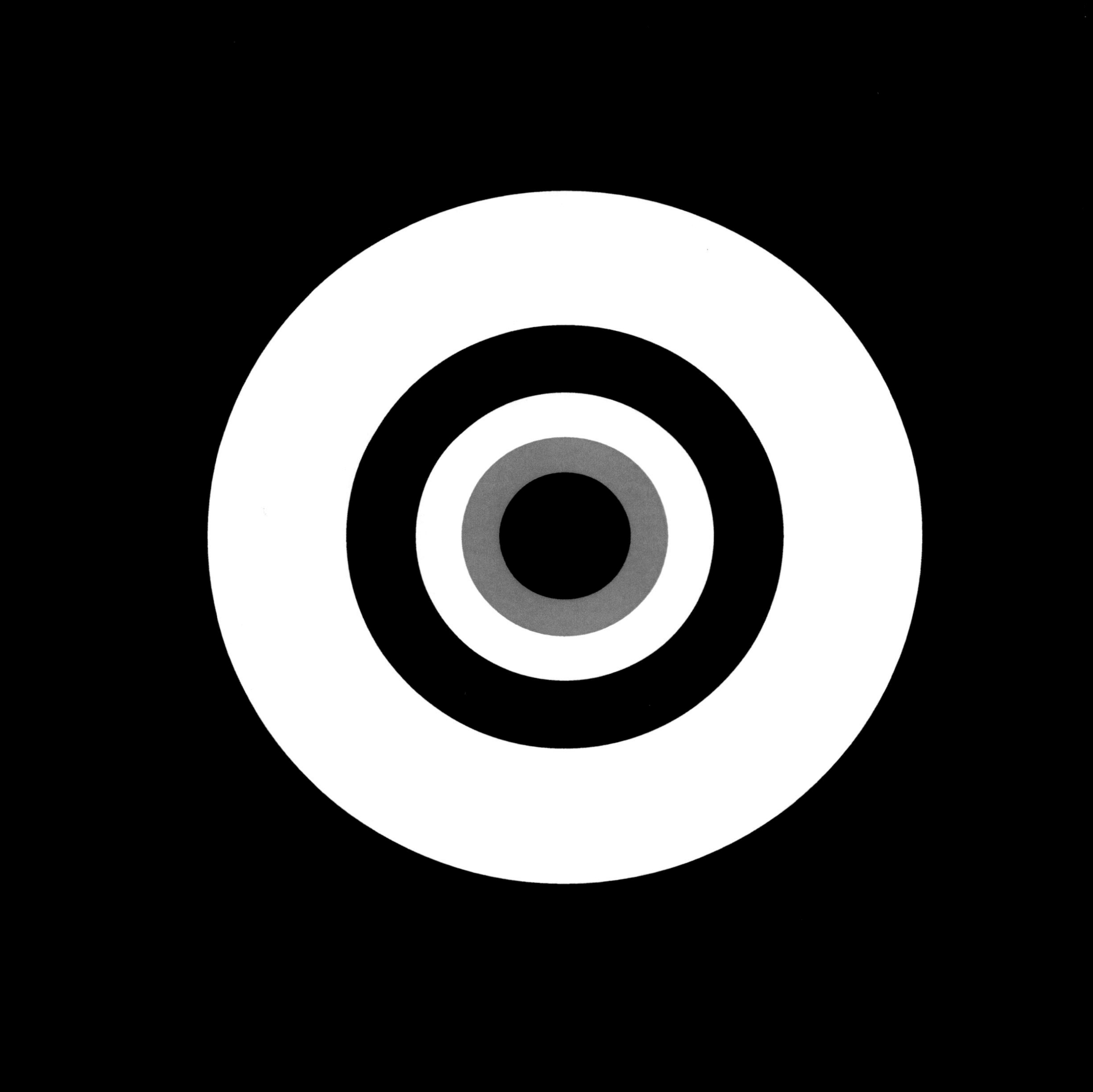

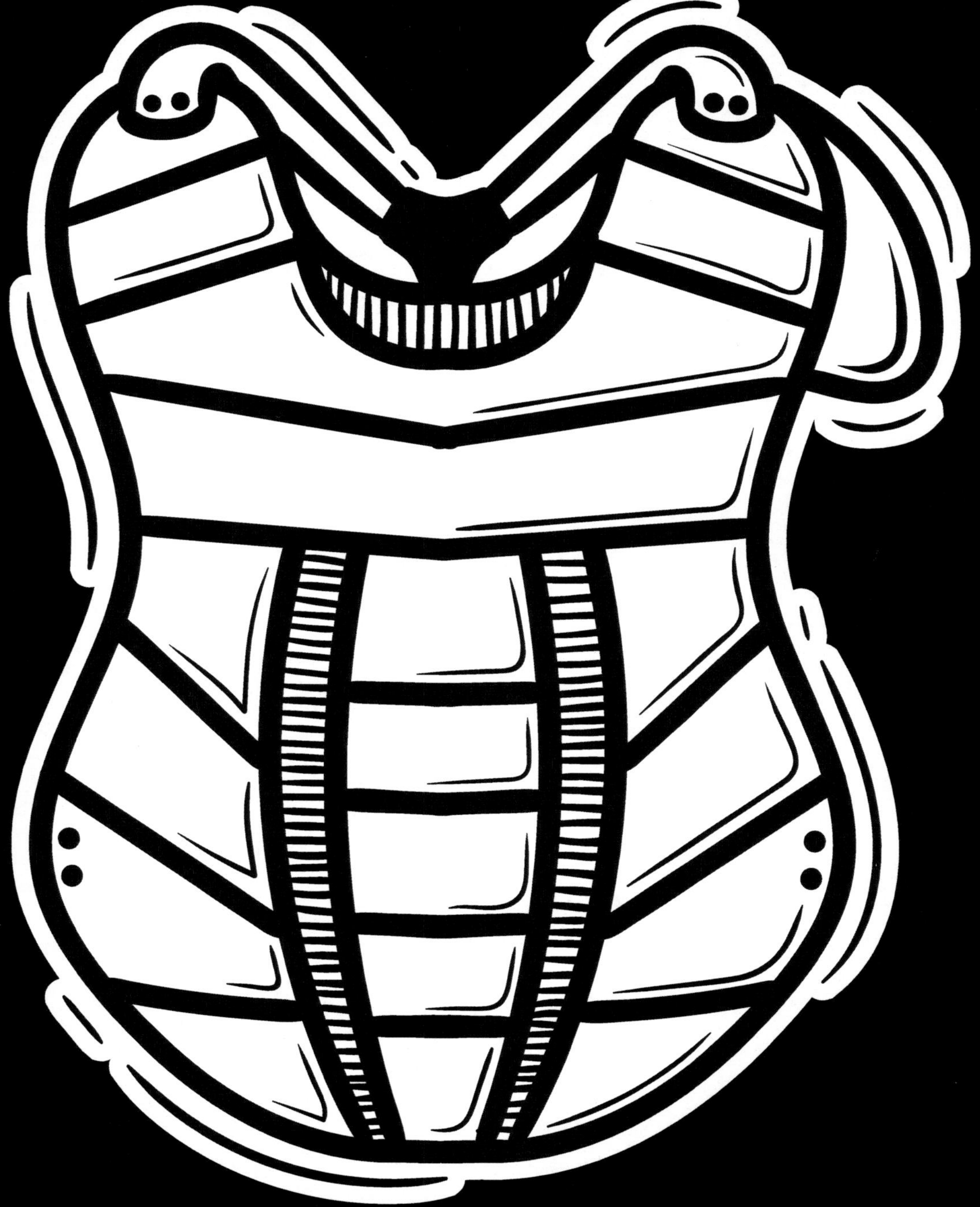

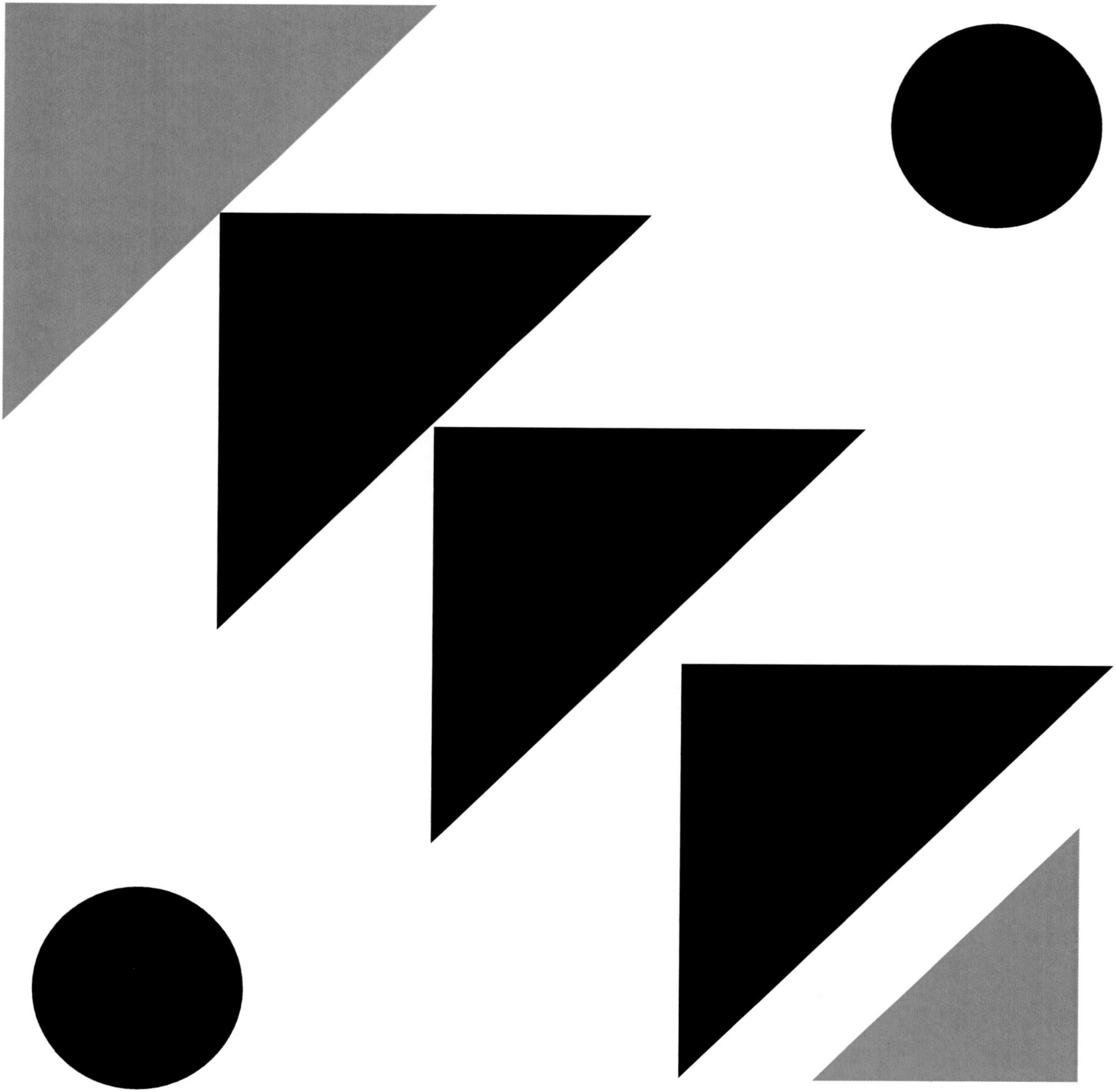

PLAY BALL

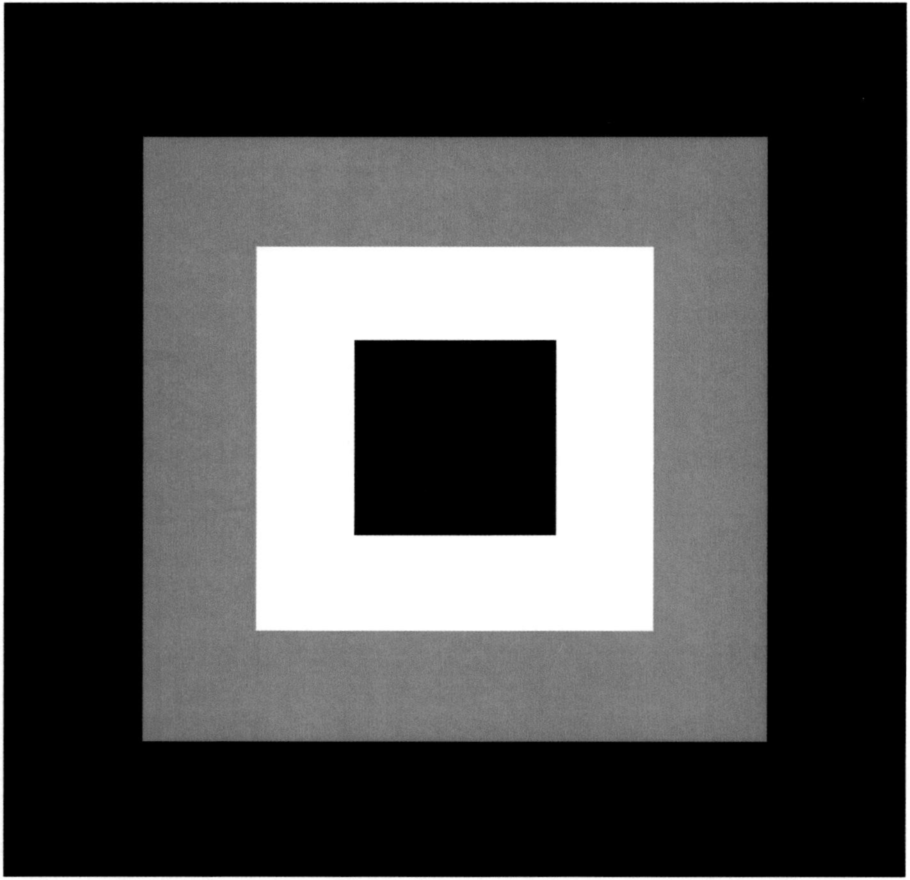

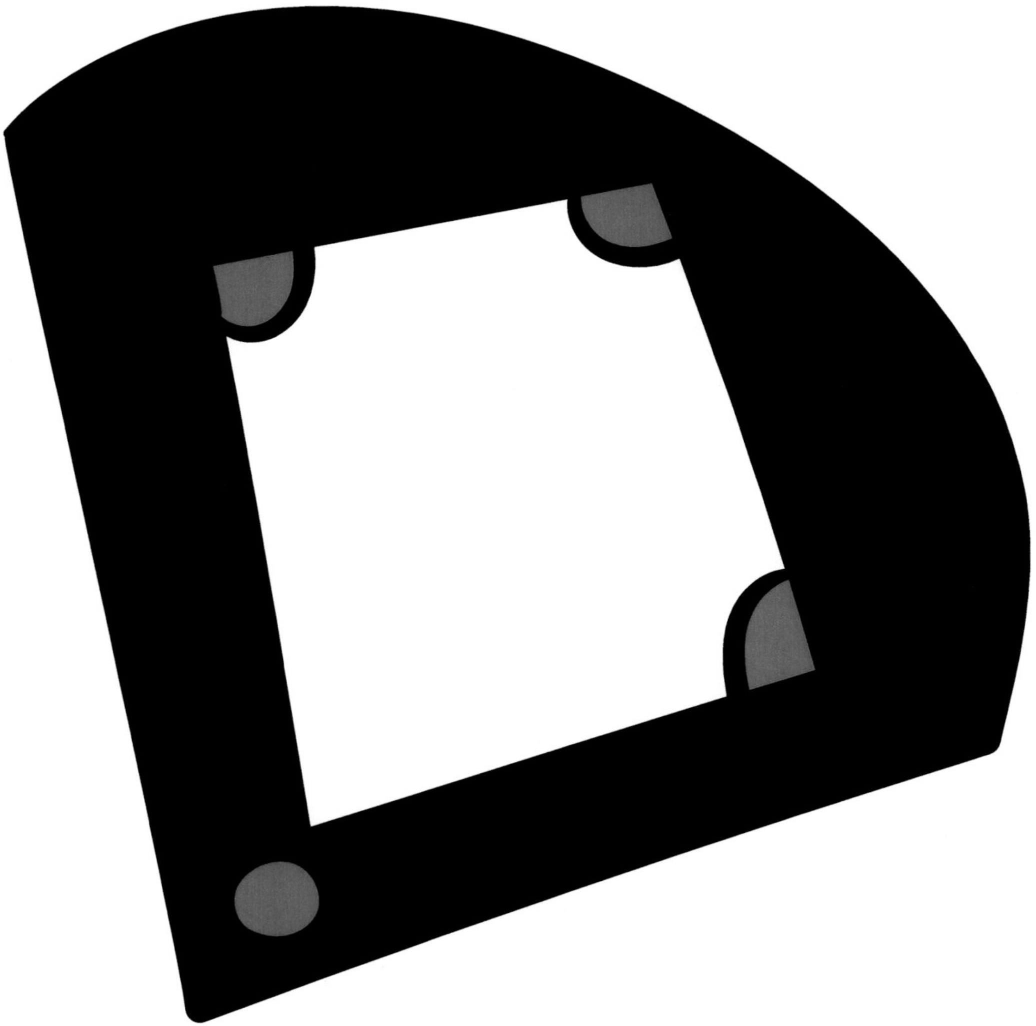

HOME RUN!

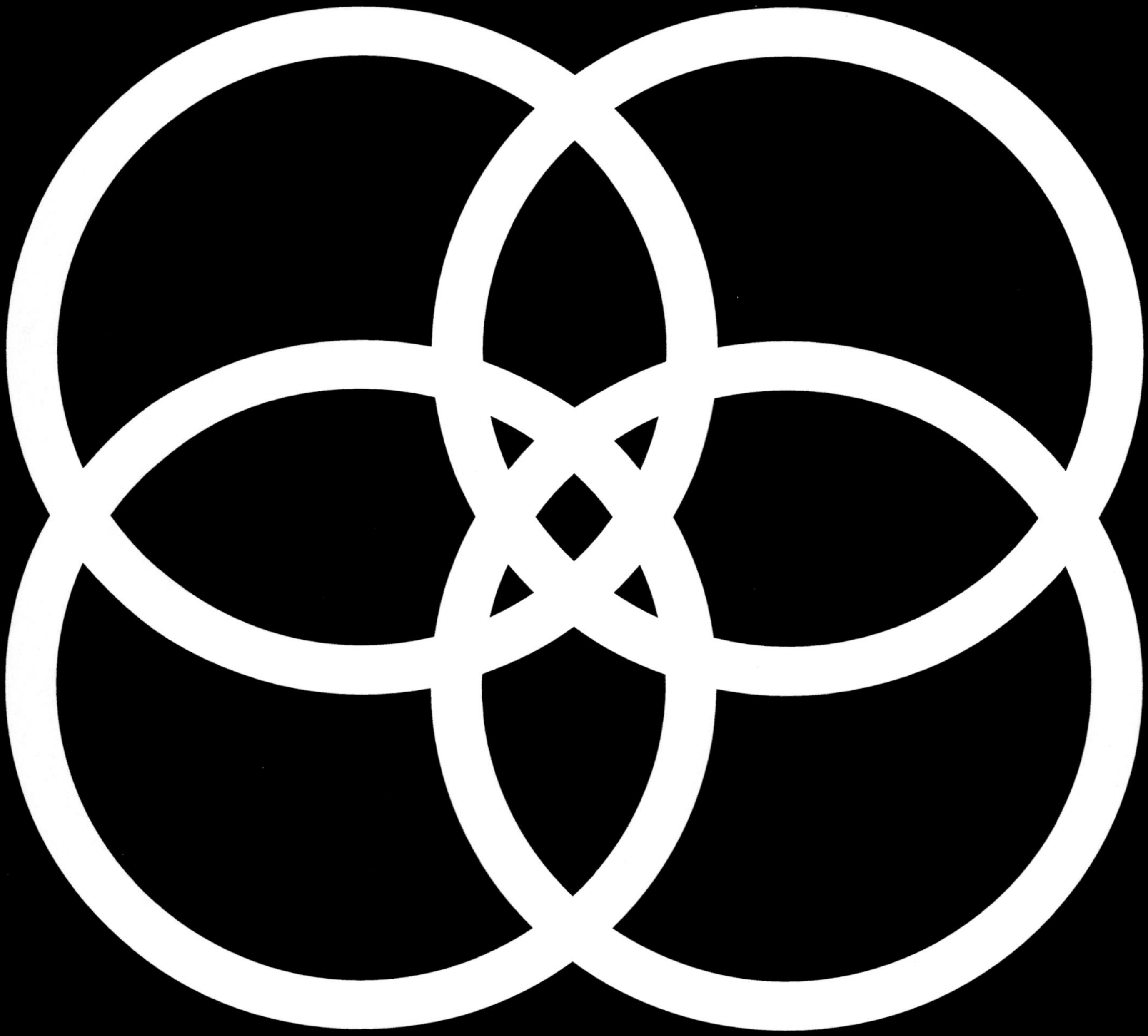

#1
STRIKE OUT!

WHAM!

POP!

1
WALK-OFF!

1

WHERE IMAGINATION FLOWS
LEARNING GROWS!
BOBO Happy

Made in United States
Orlando, FL
07 January 2024

42215497R00018